Exciting
NEW WAYS WITH
VEGETABLES

KÖNEMANN

–ASPARAGUS–

This aristocrat of the vegetable world has been prized by epicures for thousands of years. Paintings of asparagus plants have been found in Egyptian tombs 5,000 years old. Fortunately for us, asparagus is still around and good supplies of fresh asparagus spears appear at the fruit and vegetable markets for quite a reasonable price.

There are two main forms available: the thick white asparagus that is preferred by the French for its tenderness and delicate flavor, and the slender green asparagus which is less fibrous than the white and has a more pronounced flavor.

ON THE SIDE

Asparagus with Thai Dressing

Preparation time:
  8 minutes
Cooking time:
  6 minutes
Serves 6 to 8

2 bunches fresh
  asparagus (1½ to 2 lbs.)
1 small onion, sliced and
  separated into rings
½ cup chopped fresh mint
½ cup chopped cilantro
⅓ cup vegetable oil
1 tablespoon lime or
  lemon juice
1 tablespoon bottled fish
  sauce
Pinch dried red pepper
  flakes
Lettuce leaves

1 Trim asparagus and diagonally slice into 3-inch lengths. Steam over simmering water in a covered saucepan for 4 to 8 minutes or till just tender. Drain in a colander and rinse with cold water. Drain well on paper towels.
2 Toss asparagus with onion slices, mint, and cilantro. Cover and chill for 2 to 3 hours before serving.
3 In a bowl stir together oil, lime or lemon juice, fish sauce, and red pepper flakes; pour over asparagus and arrange on lettuce-lined plates.

2

Asparagus with Thai Dressing.

ASPARAGUS TIPS

Tender green asparagus tips are delicious in omelettes and quiches or served as part of a salad. They can also be stir-fried until crisp-tender. The high heat quickly cooks the vegetables and retains maximum flavor.

CHOOSING ASPARAGUS

Select firm stalks. The cut end should be moist and the tips compact and closed. Store asparagus covered in the refrigerator, standing in a little water if you aren't planning to use them at once.

PEELING ASPARAGUS

If you've purchased asparagus with thick, tough stalks, peel the lower parts of the stalks with a vegetable peeler until you reach the soft interior. Cook as usual and the stalks will taste as tender as the tips.

MEAL IN ITSELF

Veal Oscar with Lemon Sauce

Preparation time:
  15 minutes
Cooking time:
  30 minutes
Serves 4

12 asparagus spears
8 large fresh shrimp or
  prawns, shelled and
  deveined
4 veal steaks, trimmed of
  fat
All-purpose flour
2 tablespoons butter or
  margarine
1/2 cup chicken broth
1/2 cup light cream or
  evaporated skim milk
2 egg yolks
1 tablespoon lemon juice
2 tablespoons butter or
  margarine
1 tablespoon chopped
  chives

1 Drop asparagus into boiling water and cook for 4 to 8 minutes or till just tender. Drain in a colander and rinse with cold water. Cut off hard ends of asparagus. Cook shrimp or prawns in boiling water for 3 to 5 minutes or till pink. Drain; set aside.
2 Pound veal steaks till thin. Toss in flour and shake off excess. In a large skillet melt 2 tablespoons butter or margarine. Cook veal in hot butter for 4 to 5 minutes on each side or till tender. Remove from skillet and keep warm. Clean skillet.
3 For lemon sauce, in clean skillet combine chicken broth, cream or evaporated milk, egg yolks, and lemon juice. Cook and stir over low heat till heated through (do not boil). Gradually stir in 2 tablespoons butter or margarine. Cook and stir constantly till mixture slightly thickens without boiling. Add chives. Season to taste.
4 Top each veal steak with three asparagus spears and two shrimp or prawns. Spoon lemon sauce over.

CANNED ASPARAGUS

Avoid damaging the delicate tips of canned asparagus by opening the can from the bottom rather than the top.

SLICING MADE EASY

When slicing raw vegetables, it sometimes helps to cut one side off to form a steady base. Or, place the vegetable on a damp kitchen towel or paper towel to hold it in place.

COOKING ASPARAGUS

Asparagus is best cooked in a large pan standing in bunches in about 1 1/2 inches of water. Bring water to a boil, add the asparagus bunch, and cover and cook till tender. If the asparagus tips poke above the rim of the pan, improvise with a foil cover.

The Romans used to say if they wanted to do something in a hurry "Do it in less time than it takes to cook asparagus". This best describes the need to cook asparagus briefly until tender but still firm. Test thin asparagus after cooking for 4 or 5 minutes, thick asparagus after 8 minutes. It is served hot with melted butter or hollandaise sauce or cooked and served cold with vinaigrette.

Asparagus is also used in soups, quiches, soufflés, and as a garnish.

–*BEANS*–

Green or snap beans used to be known as string beans because their strings had to be removed. In many instances these have been improved by breeding so that now they snap clean and when young and tender, need only to be topped and tailed before cooking. They are available fresh all year round.

ON THE SIDE

Green Beans in a Zesty Sauce

Preparation time:
  5 minutes
Cooking time:
  14 minutes
Serves 4

1 pound fresh green
  beans
2 tablespoons butter or
  margarine
1 teaspoon
  Worcestershire sauce
1 teaspoon lemon
  juice
Shredded lemon peel

1 Trim beans and cut into 2-inch lengths. Drop into boiling water; cook 10 to 12 minutes or till tender. (Or, place in casserole with 1/4 cup water and cook, covered, on 100% power (high) for 8 to 10 minutes or till tender.) Drain; rinse in cold water.
2 In a saucepan melt butter or margarine. Add Worcestershire sauce, lemon juice, and beans. Cook and stir for 1 to 2 minutes or till beans are heated and well coated with butter mixture. Season to taste. Garnish with lemon peel.

Beans with Satay Dressing

Preparation time:
  5 minutes
Cooking time:
  12 minutes
Serves 4 to 6

8 ounces fresh green
  beans
1/3 cup salted peanuts
1/4 cup light soy
  sauce
1 tablespoon sugar
Chicken broth

1 Trim beans. Drop beans into boiling water and cook for 10 to 12 minutes or till tender. (Or, place in a microwave-safe casserole with 1/4 cup water and cook, covered, on 100% power (high) 8 to 10 minutes or till tender.) Drain in a colander and rinse with cold water. Pat dry on paper towels.
2 Cut beans diagonally into long, thin slices. Cover and chill till serving time.
3 Place peanuts in a food processor and process till finely ground. Add soy sauce and sugar. Cover and process till well combined. Blend in enough chicken broth to make a spooning consistency. Serve beans with peanut mixture.

Oriental Beans

Preparation time:
 8 minutes
Cooking time:
 17 minutes
Serves 6

1¹/2 *pounds fresh green*
 beans
¹/4 *cup cooking oil*
1 *teaspoon grated ginger*
 root
2 *cloves garlic, crushed*
8-*ounce can water*
 chestnuts, drained and
 halved
1 *stalk celery, sliced*
1 *small fresh red chili*
 pepper, seeded and
 sliced
¹/3 *cup chicken broth*

BEAN STORY

Native to Central America, green beans were introduced into Europe, where they are known as French beans. Enjoyed world wide, bean varieties include scarlet runners, golden beans, Haricot verts, Italian green beans, and the yard-long snake beans or Chinese long beans which are popular in South East Asian cooking. When cut into shorter lengths, the snake bean's quick cooking qualities and exquisite flavor make them an asset to any fast stir-fried dish.

Clockwise from top left:
Green Beans in a Zesty
Sauce, Oriental Beans and
Beans with Satay Dressing.

1 Trim beans. In a large skillet or wok heat oil. Add ginger root and garlic and stir-fry for 1 minute. Add water chestnuts and celery and stir-fry for 2 minutes or till celery is crisp-tender. Remove water chestnut mixture from skillet with a slotted spoon.
2 Add beans and chili pepper to hot skillet or wok and stir-fry for 1 minute. Add chicken broth. Bring to a boil; reduce heat. Cover and simmer for 8 to 10 minutes or till beans are crisp-tender. Return water chestnut mixture to skillet. Cook and stir for 1 to 2 minutes or till heated through.

–BELL PEPPERS–

Bell peppers come in a variety of colors such as green, red, yellow, orange, purple, and black. Their shape may be rectangular, chunky, or tapering to a point.

Native to tropical America, the bell pepper is now widely grown and used in most cuisines. It has a distinct but mild sweet-spicy taste. The riper the fruit, the higher the content of vitamins and minerals.

It is served as a vegetable either cooked or eaten raw in salads. Green bell peppers are best cooked briefly to retain their bright green color and crispness. Red-skinned varieties retain their color well and are more attractive than green peppers when in used in dishes that require longer cooking.

Peperonata

Preparation time:
  5 minutes
Cooking time:
  48 minutes
Makes 6 cups

^{1}/3 cup olive oil
4 large onions, thickly sliced and separated into rings
5 red bell peppers, cut into strips
^{2}/3 cup water
^{2}/3 cup chopped parsley
4 cloves garlic, sliced
^{1}/4 cup drained capers
^{1}/4 cup white wine vinegar
1 tablespoon sugar

1 In a large saucepan or Dutch oven heat oil. Cook onion in hot oil till tender. Add red bell peppers and water. Bring to boil; reduce heat. Simmer, uncovered, about 20 minutes or till peppers are very tender, stirring occasionally.
2 Stir in parsley, garlic, capers, vinegar, and sugar. Bring to a boil; reduce heat. Simmer, uncovered, for 10 to 15 minutes or till mixture is syrupy. Season to taste.
3 Cool slightly; spoon into clean, warm jars. Seal, label and date. Store in refrigerator. Serve at room temperature.

Peperonata.

2 tablespoons cider
  vinegar
1 cup shredded
  mozzarella cheese
1 tablespoon grated
  Parmesan cheese
Paprika

1 Halve peppers
lengthwise and remove
seeds. Drop into boiling
water for 2 to 3 minutes.
(Or, place in a
microwave-safe
casserole with ¼ cup
water and cook,
covered, on 100%
power (high) for 1 to
2 minutes.) Drain; rinse
with cold water.
2 In a large saucepan
heat oil. Cook onion
and celery in hot oil for
2 to 3 minutes or till
onion is golden brown.
Stir in cooked orzo,
tuna, olives, eggs, and
vinegar. Season to taste.
3 Fill pepper halves
with tuna mixture.
Combine cheeses;
sprinkle over filling.
Sprinkle lightly with
paprika. Place filled
peppers on a baking
sheet. Bake, uncovered,
in a 350° oven for
25 to 30 minutes or till
heated through. (Or,
place peppers on a
microwave-safe plate
and cook, uncovered, on
50% power (medium)
for 10 minutes.)

MEAL IN ITSELF

Peppers filled with Tuna and Pasta

Preparation time:
  8 minutes
Cooking time:
  36 minutes
Serves 6

3 large green bell
  peppers
1 tablespoon olive oil
1 onion, finely chopped
1 stalk celery, finely
  chopped
2 cups cooked orzo
2 x 7-ounce cans tuna,
  drained
¼ cup chopped pitted
  ripe olives
2 hard-cooked eggs,
  quartered

–*BROCCOLI*–

Broccoli with Horseradish.

Broccoli originally came from southern Europe and was well known by the ancient Romans. It owes its present popularity to the United States where it has been widely grown only since 1900.

Heads of broccoli are actually fully developed green flower buds on short fleshy stems. There are some varieties with a purplish tint. Select deep green, tightly packed bud clusters with firm stalks. The more tender leaves and fleshy stalks may also be eaten. Small flowerets can be used in soups and salads.

Broccoli stalks, peeled sliced, and sautéed, make an interesting vegetable accompaniment, or if steamed lightly, make an ideal substitute for fresh asparagus in flans.

As a vegetable, it is served raw or cooked. It is delicious steamed and served with melted butter, hollandaise sauce, or béarnaise sauce. Do not overcook. If broccoli is cooked for too long it will discolor and turn an unappetizing yellowish green color.

To store, place unwashed broccoli in the crisper section of the refrigerator or in a covered container in the lower section of the refrigerator. If it turns yellow, use immediately.

ON THE SIDE

Broccoli with Horseradish

Preparation time:
  6 minutes
Cooking time:
  10 minutes
Serves 6

1 cup mayonnaise or
  salad dressing
1 small onion, grated
¼ cup butter or
  margarine, melted
¼ cup prepared
  horseradish
¼ teaspoon dry
  mustard
Pinch paprika
1 large bunch broccoli
2 tablespoons butter or
  margarine, melted
1 tablespoon lemon juice

1 In a bowl stir together mayonnaise or salad dressing, onion, ¼ cup melted butter or margarine, horseradish, mustard, and paprika. Season to taste. Cover and chill till serving time.

2 Cut broccoli into flowerets and drop into boiling water. Cook for 6 to 8 minutes or till broccoli is tender (Or, place in a microwave-safe casserole with ¼ cup water and cook, covered, on 100% power (high) for 5 to 6 minutes or till tender.) Drain.

3 Toss warm broccoli with 2 tablespoons melted butter and lemon juice till well coated. Serve with chilled horseradish mixture.

Broccoli and Two Cheese Strudel

Preparation time:
  20 to 30 minutes
Cooking time:
  45 minutes
Serves 4 to 6

1 medium bunch
  broccoli, *cut into small
  flowerets (3 cups)*
$^1/_2$ *small head
  cauliflower, cut into
  small flowerets (2 cups)*
2 tablespoons butter or
  margarine
1 onion, finely chopped
1 clove garlic, crushed
$^1/_4$ cup all-purpose flour
1 teaspoon dried dillweed
$^1/_4$ teaspoon white pepper
Dash salt
$1^1/_4$ cups milk
$^1/_4$ cup grated Parmesan
  cheese
$1^1/_4$ cups shredded
  mozzarella cheese
8 sheets frozen phyllo
  dough, thawed
$^1/_4$ cup butter or
  margarine, melted

Broccoli and Two Cheese Strudel.

1 Cook broccoli and cauliflower flowerets in boiling water for 8 to 10 minutes or till tender. (Or, place in a microwave-safe casserole with $^1/_4$ cup water and cook, covered, on 100% power (high) for 6 to 7 minutes or till tender.) Drain; rinse with cold water. Drain well.

2 In saucepan melt 2 tablespoons butter or margarine. Cook onion and garlic in butter till tender. Stir in flour, dillweed, pepper, and salt. Add milk all at once. Cook and stir till thickened and bubbly. Cook and stir 1 minute more. Remove from heat. Add Parmesan cheese, broccoli, and

cauliflower. Stir in mozzarella cheese.
3 Brush one sheet of phyllo dough with some of the $^1/_4$ cup melted butter. Place another sheet on top and brush with more butter. Repeat till all sheets are stacked and brushed with butter. Place broccoli mixture along one side of long side of the phyllo dough,

Place 2 cups vegetables in a microwave-safe casserole with ¼ cup water. Cover and cook on 100% power (high) for 2 minutes. Drain and plunge vegetables into ice water. Drain again. The blanched vegetables can be frozen or used immediately.

CRISPY CRUNCHY CRUDITÉS

Raw, sliced, or lightly blanched vegetables served with a creamy dip make a delicious appetizer. Broccoli is a colorful addition. Simply trim leaves, wash broccoli under cold running water and cut into bite-size flowerets.

GARDEN FRESH VISITORS

If you grow your own vegetables, make sure there are no bugs hiding in your freshly picked produce by soaking it for 30 minutes in cold water with a tablespoon of vinegar.

SIMMER SENSE

If you need to add more water to simmering vegetables, use hot water. Cold water may toughen the fibers.

leaving a 2-inch border along the edge.
4 Fold short ends of phyllo in and roll up the long side. Seal dough and brush with remaining melted butter. Place roll, seam side down, in an ungreased shallow baking pan. Bake, uncovered, in 400° oven for 30 minutes or until golden brown. Let stand 10 minutes before slicing to serve.

HANDY HINT

One sheet of frozen puff pastry can be used to replace the phyllo dough. Thaw the puff pastry and roll it out to an 11x10-inch rectangle. Continue as directed for the phyllo dough.

–*CARROTS*–

Carrots have been used for at least 2,000 years and are now enjoyed throughout the world as one of the foundation vegetables for soups, stews, and casseroles. Their wonderful rich orange color and agreeable texture make them one of the most popular vegetables to be cooked and served as an accompaniment to main dishes or raw in salads.

Carrots are extremely nutritious and usually inexpensive. They have a high carotene content, vitamin content, and a good supply of minerals. They also have a high sugar content which is probably one of the reasons children eat them raw with pleasure.

Carrot and Feta Flan

Preparation time:
 20 minutes
Cooking time:
 48 minutes
Serves 6

4 slices bacon
2 onions, chopped
1 large carrot, shredded
5 sheets frozen phyllo
 dough, thawed
1/3 cup butter, melted
4 ounces feta cheese,
3 eggs
1 1/2 cups milk
3/4 cup shredded cheddar
 cheese

1 In a large skillet cook bacon till crisp. Drain bacon on a paper towel; crumble when cool. Discard bacon drippings, reserving 1 tablespoon. Cook onions and carrot in reserved drippings till onion is tender. Set aside.
2 Brush half of each phyllo sheet with melted butter. Fold each sheet of phyllo dough in half, buttered side in, to make 5 double layers. Place 1 double layer in a greased 9-inch round flan or quiche dish, allowing corners to extend over the edges. Brush dough with melted butter. Place the second double layer of dough across the first,

Carrot Soup.

staggering the corners to form points around the dish. Brush with more melted butter. Repeat until all sheets are used to form the flan shell.
3 Spread the onion mixture and bacon over the shell and sprinkle with crumbled feta cheese. Beat together eggs and milk and gently pour over filling. Sprinkle with cheddar cheese. Bake, uncovered, in a 350° oven for 30 to 40 minutes or till firm. Stand 10 minutes before cutting. Serve hot or warm with a crisp green salad or crusty bread.

Carrot Soup

Preparation time:
12 minutes
Cooking time:
33 minutes
Serves 4

2 *tablespoons butter or margarine*
6 *carrots, sliced*
1 *onion, chopped*
1 *clove garlic, crushed*
2 *medium potatoes, diced*
5 *cups chicken broth*
1 *cup sour cream or plain yogurt*
Fresh herbs

1 In a large saucepan melt butter. Add carrots, onion, and garlic and cook for 2 to 3 minutes. Stir in potatoes; reduce heat to low. Cover and cook for 4 to 5 minutes.
2 Add chicken broth to saucepan. Bring to a boil; reduce heat. Cover and simmer for 25 minutes.
3 Purée soup in a food processor or blender till smooth. Season to taste. Serve in soup bowls and dollop each serving with sour cream or yogurt and garnish with herbs.

SOMETHING SWEET

Coffee Carrot Cake with Caramel Icing

Preparation time:
  20 minutes
Cooking time:
  30 minutes
Serves 9 to 12

2/3 cup golden raisins
2/3 cup water
1 tablespoon instant
  coffee powder
6 tablespoons butter or
  margarine
1 1/4 cups packed brown
  sugar
1 teaspoon vanilla
1 egg
2 cups self-rising flour
1/2 teaspoon ground
  cinnamon
1/2 teaspoon baking soda
2 small carrots,
  shredded

Caramel Icing
1/4 cup packed brown
  sugar
2 tablespoons butter or
  margarine
1 tablespoon milk
1 1/4 cups sifted powdered
  sugar

1/3 cup chopped pecans

1 Grease and flour a
9 x 9 x 2-inch baking
pan. In a saucepan
combine raisins, water,
and coffee powder. Bring
to a boil; remove from
heat. Cool raisin mixture
to room temperature.

2 In a mixing bowl beat
butter or margarine with
an electric mixer till
softened. Beat in brown
sugar and vanilla till well
combined. Beat in egg.
Combine flour,
cinnamon, and baking
soda. Alternately fold
flour mixture and raisin
mixture into beaten
mixture. Stir in carrots.
3 Spread mixture in
prepared pan. Bake,
uncovered, in a 350°
oven about 45 minutes.
Cool slightly.
4 To make icing, in a
saucepan combine
brown sugar, butter or
margarine, and milk.
Cook and stir till smooth
(do not boil). Gradually
stir in powdered sugar
till smooth. Add
additional milk, if
necessary, to make
spreading consistency.
Spread with Caramel
Icing and sprinkle with
pecans. Cool in pan
before cutting.

JULIENNE STRIPS

To make julienne strips,
cut the carrots in half
crosswise, then in half
lengthwise. Continue
cutting the carrots
lengthwise to create
long, thin strips.

CUBING CARROTS

Use a sharp knife to cut
carrot into strips about
1/2-inch wide. Then cut
the carrot crosswise to
make cubes 1/2-inch wide
on all sides.

DICING CARROTS

Cut the same as for
cubing carrots, but
make the pieces smaller.
Ingredients that are
diced are cut into
1/4-inch pieces.

TENDER SWEET CARROTS

Carrots are most tender
and sweet when young.
As vitamins are closest
to the surface, scrub skin
with a hard vegetable
brush or peel very thinly.
Cut into slices, julienne
strips, or leave whole if
the carrots are small.
Grate coarsely to use in
salads. Carrots are
delicious in sweet recipes
as we have discovered in
the popular carrot cake.

–CAULIFLOWER–

History tells us that cauliflower was grown in the Middle East as early as the 6th century BC and was popular in Europe by the 16th century. Like its cousin, broccoli, cauliflower is cultivated for its undeveloped flowers on short stems. It is a rich source of calcium. The best cauliflower has small tightly packed white heads and fresh, juicy green leaves.

When cooking whole cauliflower, trim the tough outside leaves leaving a few tender leaves around the head to keep flowerets intact while cooking. Cauliflower is often served au gratin. Separate flowerets are used raw in salads. Blanch flowerets in boiling salted water. Drain and rinse under cold running water and dry well.

Cauliflower that has been damaged in handling or is spotted should be cooked as soon as possible before it deteriorates further.

To store cauliflower, remove the outer green leaves and wrap loosely in plastic wrap or place in a large plastic bag with a tight seal. Store in the crisper section or lower shelf of the refrigerator.

17

Cauliflower Dumplings with Tomato Sauce

Preparation time:
  1 hour
Cooking time:
  15 to 20 minutes
Serves 4 to 6

Tomato Sauce
8 large ripe tomatoes, peeled and puréed
2 tablespoons butter or margarine
1 tablespoon brown sugar
2 teaspoons paprika
1 teaspoon dried basil, crushed
1 bay leaf

Dumplings
1 medium head cauliflower
1/2 cup soy flour
1/2 teaspoon ground cumin
1/2 teaspoon dried coriander
1/2 teaspoon turmeric
1/8 teaspoon salt
1/8 teaspoon ground ginger
1/8 teaspoon ground red pepper
1 egg, lightly beaten
1 to 11/2 cups cooking oil

1 For the sauce, in a large saucepan combine puréed tomatoes, butter or margarine, brown sugar, paprika, basil, and bay leaf. Bring to a boil; reduce heat. Simmer, uncovered, for 30 to 40 minutes or until the mixture thickens. Season to taste. Keep warm till serving time.

2 For the dumplings, in a bowl combine soy flour, cumin, coriander, turmeric, salt, ginger, and red pepper. Using a food processor, finely shred cauliflower. Stir together cauliflower and soy flour mixture. Stir in egg till well combined.

3 Heat oil in a large skillet. Form cauliflower mixture into 11/2-inch balls. Cook balls in hot oil for 6 to 8 minutes or till firm and golden brown, turning to brown evenly. Drain on paper towels.

4 Arrange dumplings on individual serving plates. Pour tomato sauce over dumplings.

COOKING CAULIFLOWER

It has been said that the unappealing aroma that comes from cooking cauliflower will be reduced if you drop unshelled walnuts into the cooking water.

Cauliflower Dumplings with Tomato Sauce.

VEGETARIAN

Cauliflower Curry with Parsley Brown Rice

Preparation time:
  20 minutes
Cooking time:
  18 minutes
Serves 4 to 6

1/3 cup cooking oil
1 teaspoon finely
  shredded ginger root
1 clove garlic, crushed
1/2 teaspoon each
  ground coriander,
  cumin, and turmeric
1/2 teaspoon mustard
  seed
1/4 teaspoon ground red
  pepper
1 medium head
  cauliflower, cut into
  small flowerets
1 1/2 cups water or
  vegetable broth
1 1/4 cups frozen peas
2 ripe tomatoes,
  chopped or 1 1/4 cups
  canned tomatoes,
  chopped, and drained
1/4 cup chopped parsley
2/3 cup toasted cashews
  or other nuts

Assorted condiments
  such as sliced bananas,
  plain yogurt, toasted
  shredded coconut,
  diced red and green
  bell pepper, and
  pineapple pieces

1 In a large saucepan heat oil. Add ginger root, garlic, and spices. Cook and stir over low heat till warm, but not brown.
2 Add cauliflower and water or broth. Bring to a boil; reduce heat. Cover and simmer for 10 minutes or till cauliflower is crisp-tender.
3 Stir in frozen peas, tomatoes, and parsley. Cook, uncovered, for 4 to 5 minutes or till peas are tender. Add nuts and serve with condiments and Parsley Brown Rice.

Parsley Brown Rice
2 cups quick-cooking
  brown rice
1 bunch parsley,
  stemmed and chopped
1 tablespoon finely
  shredded lemon peel
1/2 teaspoon coarsely
  cracked pepper

Cook rice according to package directions. Toss hot rice with parsley, lemon peel, and pepper.

Cauliflower Curry with Parsley Brown Rice.

ON THE SIDE

Cauliflower and Tomato Gratin

Preparation time:
  15 minutes
Cooking time:
  30 minutes
Serves 8

1 *head cauliflower, cut into flowerets*
1 *pound tomatoes, cored, peeled and coarsely chopped*
Salt and pepper
7 *tablespoons butter or margarine, melted*
2/3 *cup fresh bread crumbs*
2/3 *cup shredded cheddar cheese*
2/3 *cup grated Parmesan cheese*

1 Cook the cauliflower in boiling salted water for 10 minutes or till crisp-tender. Drain; rinse with cold water.
2 In a greased 13 x 9 x 2-inch baking dish combine cauliflower and tomatoes. Season with salt and pepper. Drizzle half the butter over cauliflower mixture. Combine bread crumbs and cheeses; sprinkle over the cauliflower mixture. Drizzle with the remaining butter.
3 Bake, uncovered, in a 375°oven for 30 minutes or until gratin is bubbly.

–CORN–

Corn is native to tropical America and was a staple food of the Indians. Since its introduction into Europe by Columbus, its popularity has spread to all areas of the world. Corn purchased right after picking will be at its best for flavor. Look for ears with tight husks and a good tip cover. Avoid buying corn with insects or other damage or many underdeveloped kernels. The corn kernels should be firm and smooth to the touch and moist in the center. If the corn is dry looking, do not buy it since the kernels will be tough and woody.

To store corn, place on the upper shelf in the refrigerator in a brown paper bag. Corn is best cooked on the day of purchase or stored for no longer than 2 days. Instead of storing uncooked corn for longer, it is best cooked till tender, drained, and cooled quickly. Then wrap the corn in plastic wrap and store in the refrigerator for up to 2 days. To reheat, simply unwrap corn and cover with boiling water till heated through.

Corn-on-the-cob is undoubtedly the most popular way of serving sweet corn. Place the corn in unsalted boiling water (salt toughens the fibers). Add a pinch of sugar to enhance the flavor. Boil for 8 minutes or till tender. Serve warm with butter or margarine and season with salt and pepper.

To grill corn, remove husks and silk and brush with butter. Wrap each ear in foil and grill about 20 minutes or till tender, turning frequently.

SUPER STARTS

Mexican Corn Soup with Lemon

Preparation time:
  8 minutes
Cooking time:
  28 minutes
Serves 6

1 small onion, chopped
1 clove garlic, chopped
2 tablespoons butter or
  margarine
2 1/2 cups fresh, canned,
  or frozen corn kernels
1/2 to 1 teaspoon chili
  powder or a few drops
  bottled hot pepper
  sauce
3 3/4 cups chicken
  broth
1 1/4 cups milk
2 eggs
1/3 cup lemon juice
Sour cream
Chopped green onions
Thin slivered lemon peel

Mexican Corn Soup with Lemon.

1 In a large saucepan cook onion and garlic in butter for 3 minutes or till golden brown. Stir in corn and chili powder or hot pepper sauce. Add chicken broth. Bring to a boil; reduce heat. Simmer, uncovered, 20 minutes.
2 Strain soup into a large bowl, reserving broth and cooked corn mixture. Place corn mixture in a food processor or blender. Cover and process or blend about 30 seconds or till coarsely smooth. Return to saucepan. Stir in reserved broth and milk. Bring to a boil; reduce heat.
3 Slightly beat together eggs and lemon juice. Slowly stir in a little of the hot soup, then return all to saucepan. Cook and stir over low heat for 1 minute (do not boil).
4 To serve, ladle soup into bowls. Dollop with sour cream and sprinkle with green onions and lemon peel.

MICROWAVE VEGETABLE

Always cook vegetables covered in the microwave oven.
By adding just a little water for cooking, microwaved vegetables will retain most of their vitamins and minerals.

–*EGGPLANT*–

Eggplant Purée

Preparation time:
 5 minutes
Cooking time:
 1 hour
Serves 6 to 8

2 to 3 small to medium
 unpeeled eggplants
4 ounces cream cheese
1/4 cup plain yogurt
Juice of 1 lemon
1 tablespoon cooking oil
2 cloves garlic, crushed
Pitted ripe olives
Paprika

1 Place eggplants on a
baking sheet and cook
in a 350° oven for
1 hour.
2 Halve eggplants and
scoop out the pulp.
Place pulp in a food
processor or blender
container. Add cream
cheese, yogurt, lemon
juice, oil, and garlic.
Cover and process or
blend till smooth.
3 Place eggplant
mixture in a bowl and
chill for several hours.
To serve, place eggplant
purée in a serving bowl
or scooped out eggplant
shells. Garnish with
olives and sprinkle with
paprika.

Also known as
aubergine, the eggplant
is a close relative of the
potato. It is available
fresh all year round,
although it is more
plentiful and cheaper in
the summer.

It is a large and satin-
skinned vegetable and
comes in many different
colors, shapes, and sizes.

The oblong or purple-
black variety is probably
the best known, but
there are also white
egg-shaped eggplants
and small rounded
ones. Slender elongated
purple forms are the
most popular in South
East Asia and are used
extensively in Japanese
cooking.

Baked Eggplant and Tomatoes

Preparation time:
  12 minutes
Standing time:
  30 to 40 minutes
Cooking time:
  50 minutes
Serves 4

1 *small unpeeled
  eggplant, thinly sliced*
1 *teaspoon salt*
3 *medium tomatoes,
  thinly sliced*
1/3 *cup chopped parsley*
2 *cloves garlic, finely
  chopped*
1/4 *cup grated Parmesan
  cheese*
Parsley sprigs

1 Place eggplant in a colander and sprinkle with salt. Let stand for 30 to 40 minutes. Drain well and pat dry on paper towels.
2 In a lightly buttered 8 x 8 x 2-inch baking dish alternately layer eggplant, tomatoes, and parsley. Sprinkle garlic between the layers. Season to taste.
3 Cover and bake in a 400° oven for 30 minutes.
4 Uncover, baste with baking juices, and sprinkle with Parmesan cheese. Bake, uncovered, for 20 minutes more or till brown. Garnish with parsley sprigs.

Note: If mixture appears to be too dry during baking, add a little chicken broth or dry white wine as needed.

Baked Eggplant and Tomatoes.

CHOOSING EGGPLANT

Select young, firm, and glossy eggplants with tight skin and no soft patches. The skin of the eggplant is rich in vitamins and should be left on when cooking. Eggplants are always eaten cooked and may be sliced and fried, put in casseroles, stuffed, baked, or pickled.

–*LEEKS*–

Serves 4 to 6

7 ounces elbow macaroni
3 slices bacon
1 leek, chopped
3 tablespoons
  butter
3 tablespoons all-
  purpose flour
2¼ cups milk
1 cup shredded cheddar
  cheese
Pinch nutmeg
¼ cup grated Parmesan
  cheese
1 tablespoon fine dry
  bread crumbs
Pinch ground red pepper

1 Drop macaroni in boiling water; cook till al dente. Rinse with cold water. Drain. Place in greased shallow 10-inch round baking dish.
2 Cook bacon till crisp; drain. Reserve drippings. Cook leek in drippings until tender. Crumble bacon; add bacon and leek to macaroni.
3 In a saucepan melt butter. Stir in flour. Add milk; cook and stir till thickened. Stir in cheddar cheese and nutmeg till cheese melts.
4 Pour cheese sauce over macaroni mixture. Toss together Parmesan, bread crumbs, and red pepper; sprinkle over macaroni mixture. Bake, uncovered, in a 350° oven 25 to 30 minutes.

The leek is the national emblem of Wales and is traditionally worn on St. David's Day. The Roman Emperor Nero is said to have eaten large quantities of leeks to improve his voice. Perhaps this explains why the Welsh make such good choristers.

MEAL IN ITSELF

Macaroni with Leeks and Bacon

Preparation time:
  15 minutes
Cooking time:
  1 hour

Macaroni with Leeks and Bacon.

VEGETARIAN

Leeks with Savory Rice

Preparation time:
 8 minutes
Cooking time:
 36 minutes
Serves 4

4 leeks
1 tablespoon butter or
 margarine
1 cup mushrooms,
 chopped
1/2 medium red bell
 pepper, chopped
1 clove garlic,
 crushed
1 cup quick-cooking
 brown rice
1 1/4 cups chicken broth

1 Wash and trim leeks and cut into 2-inch lengths. In a medium saucepan melt butter or margarine. Cook leeks, mushrooms, red pepper, and garlic in butter for 2 to 3 minutes.
2 Add rice and stir for 1 to 2 minutes. Add chicken broth. Bring to a boil; reduce heat. Cover and simmer for 10 minutes or till all the broth is nearly absorbed and rice is tender.

DELICIOUS LEEKS

Everyone knows that leeks are delicious in soups, stews, and savory quiches. But they are also tasty on their own. Look for young, small leeks and avoid older leeks with tough outer leaves.

Steam sliced leeks until just tender and quickly cool under cold running water to prevent overcooking.

Serve leeks arranged on a platter and sprinkle with a well-flavored vinaigrette. Chill and garnish with fresh dill before serving.

PREPARING LEEKS

The leek belongs to the onion family, but differs from its cousin by forming cylindrical, not rounded, bulbs with long, fat, and broad leaves. The flavor of a leek is more delicate than an onion.

It is mostly the white shaft of the leek that is eaten. After the roots, green tops, and outer layer are removed, the leek must be thoroughly washed to remove all traces of dirt and grit. Leeks are used in soups such as the classic Vichyssoise and Cock-a-Leekie.

SALT

Try to cook your vegetables without salt and only salt those foods that you can't enjoy without it. If you eat a lot of processed food, you should avoid using salt when you cook. Some vegetables, such as eggplant, are salted and left to drain for half an hour or so before they are cooked. The salt draws out the bitter juices that this vegetable develops, especially when it is large. Rinse the salt off under cold running water and dry thoroughly with paper towels.

–MUSHROOMS–

field mushrooms. They should be clean, pale, and show no signs of sliminess.

Mushrooms store well in the refrigerator for about 1 week. Store prepackaged mushrooms in their original container and place loose mushrooms in a brown paper bag or a damp cloth. Do not store mushrooms in plastic bags because this causes them to deteriorate more quickly. Place mushrooms in the crisper section or on the lower shelf of the refrigerator. Avoid storing too many together at once since they will sweat and become slimy.

HANDY HINTS

When preparing mushrooms, never soak in water because it ruins their texture. Wipe caps with a damp cloth or brush with a mushroom brush to remove dirt. Slice about 1/4 inch from the stem of mushrooms and serve them whole, sliced, or chopped. Do not peel mushrooms. Mushrooms are tastier, more aromatic, and more nutritious the less they are cooked.

There are many forms of edible fungi, but the varieties most abundant throughout the year are called cultivated or button mushrooms and field mushrooms. The cultivated mushroom is usually harvested young, either as a button or as a cup when the cap has partly opened. Mature field mushrooms are flat with dark brown gills and have a stronger flavor. The pale oyster mushrooms are becoming more readily available and may be eaten raw or cooked the same way as button or

Creamy Mushroom Pâté

Preparation time:
 5 minutes
Cooking time:
 3 minutes
Serves 6

8 ounces mushrooms,
 finely chopped
1 tablespoon finely
 chopped onion
1/2 cup butter or
 margarine
3-ounce container
 cream cheese, cubed
 and softened
Few drops
 Worcestershire sauce

1 In a saucepan cook
mushrooms and onion
in butter for 3 minutes
or till tender. (Or, place
in a microwave-safe
casserole and cook,
covered, on 100%
power (high) for 1 to
2 minutes or till tender.)
2 Place mushroom
mixture in a food
processor or blender.
Add cream cheese and
Worcestershire sauce.
Cover and process or
blend till smooth.
Season to taste.
3 Spoon mixture into
a crock or 6 individual
ramekins. Cool. Cover
and chill till serving
time.

Creamy Mushroom Pâté.

Broiled Mushroom Caps

Preparation time:
  15 minutes
Cooking time:
  10 minutes
Serves 6

1 *pound medium*
  mushrooms
2 *to 4 cloves garlic,*
  crushed
¼ *cup butter or*
  margarine, softened
¼ *cup grated Parmesan*
  cheese
¼ *cup soft bread*
  crumbs
4 *slices bacon*

1 Wipe mushrooms and carefully remove stems. Finely chop stems and combine them with the crushed garlic.

2 In a bowl mash butter with a fork and stir in Parmesan cheese, bread crumbs, and mushroom stalk mixture. In a small skillet cook bacon till crisp; drain on paper towel. Crumble bacon and add to cheese mixture.

3 Fill each mushroom cap with the cheese mixture. Place caps on the unheated rack of a broiler pan. Broil about 4 inches from the heat for 3 to 5 minutes or till browned and heated through.

ON THE SIDE

Marinated Mushrooms

Preparation time:
  5 minutes
Cooking time:
  8 minutes
Makes 2 cups

1 pound mushrooms
²⁄₃ cup water
1 tablespoon lemon juice
²⁄₃ cup white or red wine
  vinegar
1 small onion, finely
  chopped
1 small clove garlic, peeled
1 bay leaf
¼ cup olive oil
2 tablespoons tomato
  sauce

1 In a saucepan combine mushrooms, water, and lemon juice. Bring to a boil; reduce heat. Simmer, uncovered, for 2 to 3 minutes. Drain; transfer to a bowl.
2 In same saucepan combine vinegar, onion, garlic, and bay leaf. Bring to a boil; reduce heat. Simmer, uncovered, for 3 to 4 minutes or till onion is tender. Stir in oil and tomato sauce. Season to taste.
3 Pour vinegar mixture over mushrooms. Cover; chill overnight. Before serving, remove the garlic and bay leaf.

Marinated Mushrooms.

Chicken with Mushrooms

Preparation time:
  10 minutes
Cooking time:
  5 minutes
Serves 4

1 *pound boneless,*
  skinless chicken breasts
2 *teaspoons oyster sauce*
2 *teaspoons soy sauce*
1 *teaspoon hoisin sauce*
2 *teaspoons cornstarch*
1/2 *teaspoon sesame oil*
1/4 *cup cooking oil*
3 *shallots, coarsely*
  chopped
1 *onion, cut into thin*
  wedges
1 *cup mushrooms*

1 Cut chicken into
1/2-inch pieces. In bowl,
stir together oyster, soy,
and hoisin sauces,
cornstarch and sesame
oil. Add chicken, tossing
to coat. Stand 20 minutes.
2 In a large skillet heat
half the cooking oil over
medium-high heat. Add
shallots and onion
wedges; stir-fry 2 to 3
minutes. Add mushrooms;
stir-fry 1 minute. Remove
vegetables from skillet.
3 Add remaining oil to
skillet. Add chicken;
stir-fry over high heat
1 to 2 minutes. Return
mushroom mixture to
skillet; stir-fry 1 minute
more or till heated.

-MICROWAVE YOUR VEGETABLES -

Vegetables are all microwaved on 100% power (high), covered. Cooking times are approximate. Test before adding extra cooking time.

Vegetables	Quantity	Preparation	Cooking Time (minutes)*
Artichokes	2 medium	1/4 cup water	8-9
Asparagus, fresh	8 oz	2 tablespoons water	7-8
Asparagus, frozen	8 oz	2 tablespoons water	4-5
Beans, fresh	8 oz	1/4 cup water	7-8
Beans, frozen	8 oz	2 tablespoons water	6
Broccoli, fresh	8 oz	slit stalks, 1/4 cup water	8
Broccoli, frozen	8 oz	2 tablespoons water	6
Brussels sprouts, fresh	8 oz	2 tablespoons water	7-8
Brussels sprouts, frozen	8 oz	2 tablespoons water	6
Cabbage, shredded	1/2 small	only water remaining after washing, knob of butter and pepper	8
Carrots, fresh	4 sliced	1/4 cup water	8
Carrots, frozen	8 oz	2 tablespoons water	5-6
Cauliflower, fresh	1/2 head	slit stalks, 1/4 cup water	10
Cauliflower, frozen	8 oz	2 tablespoons water	7-8
Celery, fresh	2 cups, chopped	2 tablespoons water	6-8

Corn on the cob, fresh	2	remove husks, dot with butter, wrap in plastic wrap	5
Corn on the cob, frozen	1 lb	dot with butter	6
Eggplant, sliced	1 medium	soak in the water, drain well or press, dot with butter	5-6
Mushrooms, fresh	8oz	whole or sliced, dot with butter	3
Onions, sliced	2 medium	1 tablespoon butter	4
Parsnips, sliced	2 medium	2 tablespoons water	5-6
Peas, fresh	8 oz	2 tablespoons water	7-8
Peas, frozen	1 lb	2 tablespoons water	10
Potatoes, peeled	1 lb	cut into quarters, 1/4 cup water	8-10
Potatoes, skin on	2 medium	pierce skin, rub with oil, turn over after 3 minutes	6
Pumpkin	1 lb	cut into serving pieces, 2 tablespoons water	6
Spinach, fresh	1/2 bunch	only water remaining after washing, 1 tablespoon butter, dash nutmeg and pepper	6
Spinach, frozen	8 oz	dash nutmeg and pepper	5-6
Tomatoes, sliced	2	dot with butter, sprinkle with sugar and pepper	2-3
Tomatoes, halved	6 halves	dot with butter and pepper	3-4
Zucchini, sliced	2 medium	1 tablespoon butter and pepper	4-5

* *Note:* Cooking time is approximate. Remember, cooking times depend on how well done you like your vegetables and on the power rating of your microwave oven.

–*ONIONS*–

whole in casseroles. Choose onions that are dry with a smooth shiny skin. Avoid onions that have begun to sprout.

Pickled Onions

Preparation time:
  15 minutes
Marinating time:
  36 hours
Cooking time:
  8 minutes
Makes 2 pounds

2 pounds small white
  onions, unpeeled
2 1/4 cups salt
11 1/4 cups water
3 3/4 cups white vinegar
1 1/4 cups tarragon vinegar
1 tablespoon black
  peppercorns
1/2 teaspoon ground
  allspice
2 tablespoons brown
  sugar
2 whole cloves
1 cinnamon stick

1 Wash onions and place them in a large bowl. Mix half salt with half water and pour over onions to cover them. Place a heavy plate on top of onions to weigh them down so they are totally immersed. Let stand for 12 hours.
2 Drain and peel onions and place in clean bowl. Stir together remaining salt and water and pour

Onions have been used used as a vegetable since prehistoric times.

Onions are slightly dried before marketing, making their skins dry and paper thin. They vary in flavor from mild to strong. Yellow onions have a strong flavor and are used in soups, stews, and other prepared dishes. They keep well

and are available all year round. Red onions have a mild sweet flavor and are used in salads and sliced in rings to use as a garnish. White onions are mild and used raw in salads or quickly stir-fried in Asian dishes. Small white onions are particularly suitable for pickling or cooking

over onions. Cover as before; stand 24 hours.
3 Drain and wash onions. Pack loosely into sterilized jars.
4 In a saucepan combine vinegars, peppercorns, allspice, sugar, cloves and cinnamon stick. Bring to boil; reduce heat. Simmer, uncovered, 5 minutes.
5 Strain through a fine sieve and pour over onions, leaving at least 1/2-inch of headspace. Seal lids. Let stand for 3 months before serving.

Mustard Pickles

Preparation time:
  40 minutes
Marinating time:
  24 hours
Cooking time:
  30 minutes
Makes about 3 pounds

Pickled Onions and Mustard Pickles.

1 cup salt
1 small cucumber,
  chopped
3 onions, chopped
1 1/2 pounds tomatoes,
  coarsely chopped
1 large head cauliflower,
  washed, and cut into
  flowerets
3 1/4 cups white wine
  vinegar
2 teaspoons dry mustard
1 teaspoon each ground
  ginger, black pepper,
  and pickling spice
Few coriander seeds
1 1/4 cups brown sugar
3/4 cup golden raisins ·

1 In a large bowl alternately layer salt and vegetables Cover with cold water. Cover bowl with foil; stand in a cool place for 24 hours.
2 Rinse and thoroughly drain vegetables. In a large saucepan combine drained vegetables, vinegar, dry mustard, ginger, pepper, pickling spice, and coriander seeds. Stir in brown sugar and raisins. Cook and stir till sugar dissolves.
3 Bring to a boil; reduce heat. Simmer, uncovered, 20 minutes or till vegetables are tender, stirring occasionally. Pour into sterilized jars, leaving at least 1/2-inch of headspace. Seal lids.

37

Mexican Onions.

Mexican Onions

Preparation time:
  8 minutes
Cooking time:
  45 minutes
Serves 6

6 medium unpeeled
  onions
1 tablespoon butter
1 tablespoon all-purpose
  flour
Pinch chili powder
1/2 cup milk
1/3 cup drained canned
  corn kernels
1/3 cup shredded cheddar
  cheese

2 tablespoons chopped
  red bell pepper

1 In a large saucepan or Dutch oven bring salted water to a boil. Add onions. Return to a boil; reduce heat. Simmer, uncovered, for 10 minutes. Drain and cool slightly. Cut off the tops of the onions and remove peel. Hollow out the onions, leaving a 1/4-inch thick shell. Chop insides of onions to make 1/4 cup.
2 In a medium saucepan melt butter. Stir in flour and chili powder. Add milk all at once. Cook and stir till thickened and bubbly.

Cook and stir 1 minute more. Add corn, cheese, bell pepper, and the reserved chopped onion. Season to taste.
3 Place onions in a single layer in a shallow baking dish. Spoon corn mixture into onions, allowing some to spill over sides. Bake, uncovered, in a 400° oven for 30 minutes.

DON'T CRY

Peel onions under cold tap water to reduce the vapor in the air. It's also a good idea to keep a bowl of water nearby for wetting the pieces of onion you are slicing.

Hot Onion Salad.

Hot Onion Salad

Preparation time:
  10 minutes
Cooking time:
  1 1/2 hours
Serves 6

Sauce
14 1/2-ounce can whole
  tomatoes, drained
2 onions, coarsely
  chopped
3 cloves garlic, crushed
1 bouquet garni
1 sprig fresh basil
1/3 cup olive oil

Salad
2 pounds small white
  onions
1 1/4 cups white wine
  vinegar
2/3 cup olive oil
1/4 cup golden
  raisins
1/4 cup sugar
1 bouquet garni

1 For sauce, in a
saucepan combine
drained tomatoes,
chopped onions, garlic,
bouquet garni, and
basil. Stir in 1/3 cup olive
oil. Cook over medium
heat for 30 minutes or
till onions are tender.

Pour into a sieve and
press with a wooden
spoon to extract as
much liquid as possible.
2 For salad, peel onions
and place in a large
heavy saucepan. Add
the sauce, vinegar,
2/3 cup oil, raisins, sugar,
and bouquet garni.
Add just enough water
to cover the onions.
Bring to a boil; reduce
heat. Simmer,
uncovered, for 1 hour
or till onions are tender.
Season to taste.
Serve hot or cool
with grilled meat.

–POTATOES–

ON THE SIDE

Soufflé Potatoes

Preparation time:
  10 minutes
Cooking time:
  1 hour and 50 minutes
Serves 4

4 *large baking potatoes*
1 *cup cheddar cheese*
1/2 *cup sour cream*
2 *tablespoons chopped*
  chives or parsley
Pinch paprika
2 *egg yolks, slightly*
  beaten
3 *egg whites*

1 Wash potatoes and pierce with a fork several times. Bake in a 350° oven for 1¼ to 1½ hours or till tender. Cut a slice from the top of each potato. Gently scoop out each potato, leaving a ¼-inch shell.
2 Place scooped out potato in a bowl; mash. Add shredded cheese, sour cream, chives or parsley, and paprika. Stir in yolks. Beat whites with an electric mixer till stiff peaks form. Gently fold beaten whites into potato mixture. Spoon into shells.
3 Place potatoes on a baking sheet and bake, uncovered, in 400° oven 20 to 25 minutes or till golden brown and puffy.

Soufflé Potatoes.

The value of the potato as a staple food was discovered in prehistoric times, apparently by the Incas of Peru. Potatoes were introduced to Europe by the first Spanish explorers and now are the most widely eaten food, next to rice.

   The potato is a valuable source of dietary starch, vitamin C, amino acids, protein, thiamin, and niacin. Potatoes are sometimes perceived as fattening but it is the addition of butter and sour cream that puts on the weight. The potato itself is 99.9 per cent fat free which makes it about as fattening as a pear.
A lot of goodness is just under the skin, so leave the skins on whenever it is possible.

ON THE SIDE

Cheesy Baked Potatoes

Preparation time:
  5 minutes
Cooking time:
  47 minutes
Serves 6

6 large baking potatoes,
  peeled
Garlic salt
Paprika
6 to 8 slices American
  cheese
3 tablespoons butter

1 Halve potatoes crosswise and arrange, cut side down, in a buttered 2½- or 3-quart casserole. Sprinkle with garlic salt and paprika. Bake, uncovered, in a 350° oven for 40 minutes or till tender.
2 Cut cheese into pieces big enough to cover top of each potato. Place cheese over potatoes. Drizzle with melted butter. Return to oven and bake for 6 to 7 minutes more or till cheese melts.

VARIATION

Lay strips of ham, onion, or smoked salmon over the potatoes before topping them with the cheese.

Cheesy Baked Potatoes.

–*PUMPKIN*–

Pumpkins grow on large sprawling vines and are a member of a large vegetable family that includes melon, cucumber, zucchini, and squash.

Pumpkins have a sweet, slightly stringy pulp that can be used in recipes calling for winter squash. Whole fresh pumpkins can be purchased from September through early winter, but canned pumpkin, which is available all year long, is the form usually used in cooking.

In the United States, pumpkin pie is the traditional Thanksgiving dessert. Pumpkin is also sometimes boiled and baked and served as a side dish or mashed and used in soups.

Choose a pumpkin with a firm shiny skin and one that feels heavy in relation to its size. If serving in the pumpkin shell, choose one with an attractive shape and steady base.

SUPER STARTS

Curried Pumpkin Soup

Preparation time:
15 minutes
Cooking time:
30 minutes
Serves 4 to 6

¹/₃ cup chopped onion
1 clove garlic, crushed
1 teaspoon curry powder

Curried Pumpkin Soup.

2 tablespoons butter or
  margarine
1/2 x 16-ounce can
  pumpkin (about
  1 cup)
1/4 teaspoon ground
  nutmeg
1/8 teaspoon sugar
1 bay leaf
2 cups chicken
  broth
1 1/2 cups milk
1 tablespoon
  cornstarch
2 tablespoons heavy
  cream
Chives

1 In large saucepan cook onion, garlic, and curry powder in butter or margarine 5 minutes or till tender. Add pumpkin, nutmeg, sugar, and bay leaf. Stir in chicken broth.
2 Bring to boil; reduce heat. Simmer, uncovered, 15 minutes. Remove from heat; discard bay leaf.
3 Stir in 1 cup of the milk and cook over low heat 2 to 3 minutes or till heated. Stir together remaining milk and cornstarch. Add to hot mixture. Cook and stir till thickened and bubbly; cook 2 minutes more. To serve, swirl with cream and garnish with chives.

MEAL IN ITSELF

Pumpkin Gnocchi

Preparation time:
  10 minutes
Chilling time:
  2 hours
Cooking time:
  30 minutes
Serves 4

1 *cup milk*
1/2 *cup semolina or
  quick-cooking
  farina*
1 *cup canned pumpkin*
2 *tablespoons butter or
  margarine*
1/4 *teaspoon ground
  nutmeg*
1 *beaten egg*
1/2 *cup grated Parmesan
  cheese*
2 *tablespoons grated
  Parmesan cheese*
1/2 *cup unsalted
  butter*

Pumpkin Gnocchi.

1 Line an 8 x 8 x 2-inch baking pan with plastic wrap; set aside.
2 In medium saucepan combine milk and semolina or farina; mix well. Stir in pumpkin, butter or margarine, and nutmeg. Cook and stir over medium heat till bubbly. Cook and stir 5 minutes more or till very thick. Remove mixture from heat.
3 Stir about 1/2 cup of the hot mixture into the egg. Return all to the saucepan. Stir in 1/2 cup Parmesan cheese. Pour into prepared pan; spread evenly. Chill for 2 hours.
4 Invert pan onto a cutting surface; remove plastic wrap. Sprinkle with 2 tablespoons Parmesan cheese. Cut into 24 rectangles and place them 1/2 inch apart on a greased baking sheet.
5 Bake, uncovered, in a 425° oven for 20 to 25 minutes or till golden. Stand 5 minutes before removing from baking sheet.
6 Meanwhile, in a small saucepan melt unsalted butter over low heat till golden. Serve warm gnocchi drizzled with the brown butter.

MAKE YOUR OWN

To make your own pumpkin purée, cut a lid from the top of a fresh pumpkin. Scrape out the seeds and pulp and discard them. Replace the lid and place the pumpkin on a baking sheet in a 350° oven for 1 to 1 1/2 hours or till tender. Remove from oven and scrape out the flesh from the pumpkin. Mash the cooked pumpkin and measure out the amount you require for the recipe. If the pumpkin skin is unbroken, it can serve as a container for recipes such as our Curried Pumpkin Soup.

–SPINACH–

Spinach and Vegetable Terrine

Preparation time:
  20 minutes
Cooking time:
  1 hour and 45 minutes
Serves 6 to 8

1 leek
2 1/2 cups fresh or frozen
  peas
5 cups chopped fresh
  spinach or 10-ounce
  package frozen
1 egg
1 teaspoon dried
  tarragon, crushed
1/4 teaspoon salt
Freshly ground pepper
3 3/4 cups sliced carrots
1/4 cup all-purpose flour
1 teaspoon ground
  nutmeg
1/4 teaspoon salt
Freshly ground pepper

1 Slice white part of the leek into thin rounds. Steam 1 to 2 minutes or till tender. Line 8 x 4 x 3-inch loaf pan with waxed paper; grease paper. Arrange leek over bottom of loaf pan.
2 In a large saucepan add peas to lightly salted boiling water and place spinach leaves or thawed spinach on top of peas. Cover; cook 4 to 6 minutes or till peas are tender. Drain well, press out excess liquid.
3 In a food processor,

Fresh spinach has dark green oval to round leaves and slender green stalks. Spinach has a mild, yet hearty, flavor and can be served raw in salads or cooked.

Look for fresh spinach all year round in your grocer's produce section as well as canned and frozen. When buying fresh spinach, look for leaves that are crisp and free of moisture or mold. Avoid spinach leaves that are broken or bruised.

Spinach must always be washed well in two or three changes of water until all traces of sand and soil are removed. Pat the leaves dry with paper towels and store in a plastic bag or airtight container in the refrigerator for up to three days.

combine pea-spinach mixture, egg, tarragon, 1/4 teaspoon salt, and pepper. Cover and process till well combined. Spoon mixture over leeks in pan, smoothing the top. Cook carrots in lightly salted boiling for 12 to 15 minutes or till tender. In a food processor combine carrots, flour, nutmeg, 1/4 teaspoon salt, and pepper. Process till smooth. Spoon carrot mixture over spinach mixture; smooth top. Tap pan firmly to remove air bubbles.
4 Cover pan with waxed paper and seal tightly with aluminum foil. Bake in a 350° oven for 1 hour. Chill at least 3 hours before serving. Invert terrine onto a serving plate. Slice; serve with Tomato Sauce.

Tomato Sauce
14 1/2-ounce can whole
  tomatoes, undrained
1 small onion, chopped
1/3 cup white wine
1/4 cup tomato paste
1 clove garlic, crushed
1 tablespoon chopped
  fresh basil
Freshly ground pepper

1 Combine all ingredients. Bring to boil; reduce heat. Simmer, uncovered, 30 minutes.
2 Place tomato mixture in a food processor or blender. Cover; process till smooth. Chill.

Spinach Turnovers

Preparation time:
  30 minutes
Cooking time:
  20 minutes
Makes 24 turnovers

17¹/4-*ounce package*
  frozen puff pastry
2 x 10-*ounce packages*
  frozen spinach
1 *cup shredded cheddar*
  cheese
Pinch nutmeg
2 *egg yolks, beaten*
Juice of 1 lemon
1 *egg, beaten*
1 *tablespoon sesame seed*

1 Thaw pastry. Roll each
sheet to a 13 x 18-inch
rectangle, about ¹/8-inch
thick. Cut each sheet into
twelve 4-inch circles.
2 Drain spinach; squeeze
dry and finely chop.
Combine spinach,
shredded cheese, and
nutmeg. Add egg yolks
and lemon juice; mix well.
3 Spoon tablespoon of
spinach mixture in
middle of pastry circles.
Brush edge of pastry
with egg. Fold pastry
over spinach mixture;
press edges together to
seal. Brush pastry with
egg; sprinkle with
sesame seed.
4 Bake turnovers on
baking sheet in 400°
oven 18 to 20 minutes
or till golden brown.

Spinach Turnovers.

–SPROUTS–

The nutritional value of seed sprouts is virtually unrivaled on the basis of cost, volume, and ease of preparation. As seeds sprout, the starches stored within are released and converted into vitamins, minerals, and proteins, making them a very nutritious food. Bean sprouts and alfalfa sprouts are popular examples. They are easily grown in a clean jar and only take a few days till harvest.

SPROUTING INSTRUCTIONS

Beans and seeds increase in volume up to 10 times their original size as they sprout, so use a jar large enough to allow for this expansion.

First soak the beans for 12 hours in a glass jar. Rinse and drain off the water. Cover the mouth of the jar with a piece of cheesecloth and secure with string or a rubber band.

Lay the jar on its side in a warm environment, but not in direct sunlight. To keep the seeds moist, rinse them twice a day and drain off all the water or they will rot. Continue wetting and draining the sprouts till they are ready to eat.

Alfalfa-Avocado Crêpes

Preparation time:
  20 minutes
Cooking time:
  15 minutes
Serves 8

Crêpe Batter
3/4 cup milk
1/2 cup all-purpose flour
1 egg
2 teaspoons cooking oil
Dash salt

Filling
8 ounces cottage cheese,
  drained (1 cup)
1/3 cup shredded shallots
2 avocadoes, pitted,
  peeled, and sliced
2 cups loosely packed
  alfalfa sprouts
Melted butter

1 For crêpes, in a medium bowl combine milk, flour, egg, oil, and salt. Beat till smooth.
2 To make crêpes, heat a lightly greased 6-inch skillet. Remove from heat. Pour about 2 tablespoons batter in skillet; tilt skillet to spread batter. Return to heat and brown on one side only. Invert skillet over paper towels and remove crêpe. Repeat with remaining batter.
3 For filling, in a bowl stir together cottage cheese and shallots.

Spread over one half of light side of the cooked crêpe. Top with avocado. Fold crêpes over filling.
4 Cook filled crêpes in a skillet with butter till filling is heated through and crêpe is crisp on both sides. Sprinkle with sprouts. Serve.

Tuna and Mung Bean Pockets

Preparation time:
  10 minutes
Cooking time:
  None
Serves 4

4 ounces mung beans
1 avocado, pitted,
  peeled, and chopped
3 1/2-ounce can tuna,
  drained and flaked
1/4 cup mayonnaise
4 small pita bread rounds
1 cup loosely packed
  alfalfa sprouts

1 In a bowl combine mung beans, avocado, tuna, and mayonnaise. Cut pita bread crosswise to form 8 pockets. Spoon tuna mixture into pockets. Top with sprouts.

Chinese Beef and Vegetables

Preparation time:
  15 minutes
Cooking time:
  10 minutes

Serves 4

1/4 cup cooking oil
1 pound lean boneless
  beef, thinly sliced
1/2 cup sliced mushrooms
8 ounces bean sprouts
8-ounce can water
  chestnuts, drained
3 shallots, cut into strips
1 green or red bell
  pepper, cut into strips
1 carrot, cut into strips
1 stalk celery, cut into
  strips
2 cloves garlic, crushed
1 tablespoon finely
  shredded ginger root
2/3 cup beef broth
1 tablespoon dry sherry
2 teaspoons cornstarch
Hot cooked rice

1 Heat oil in large skillet. Cook meat, half at a time, till brown. Remove from skillet. Add mushrooms to skillet; cook 1 minute; remove.
2 Add bean sprouts, water chestnuts, shallots, bell pepper, carrot, celery, garlic, and ginger root to skillet. Cook and stir for 1 minute.
3 In a small bowl stir together beef broth, sherry, and cornstarch. Add to skillet. Cook and stir till thickened. Cook and stir 2 minutes more. Return meat and mushrooms to skillet. Cook and stir till heated through. Serve with rice.

On The Side

Gado-gado

Preparation time:
  15 minutes
Cooking time:
  3 minutes
Serves 6 to 8

2 large carrots, thinly
  sliced
6 ounces fresh green
  beans, trimmed and
  sliced diagonally
6 ounces bean sprouts
1¹/4 cups shredded
  cabbage
1 large onion, chopped
1 cucumber, thinly sliced
3 hard-cooked eggs,
  sliced

Sauce
1¹/4 cups unsalted
  peanuts
¹/2 cup sugar
¹/4 cup lemon juice or
  vinegar
3 cloves garlic, peeled
¹/4 cup chopped shallots

1 Blanch carrots and
green beans in boiling
water for 2 minutes.
Drain in a colander and
rinse with cold water.
2 Blanch bean sprouts,
cabbage, and onion in
boiling water for
1 minute. Drain in a
colander and rinse with
cold water.
3 Arrange blanched
vegetables, cucumber,
and eggs on a serving
platter. Cover and chill
till serving time.
4 For sauce, in a food
processor or blender
combine peanuts, sugar,
lemon juice or vinegar,
and garlic. Cover and
process or blend till
smooth. Season to taste.
5 To serve, drizzle sauce
over vegetable mixture
and garnish with
chopped shallots.

Radish and Alfalfa Salad

Preparation time:
  10 minutes
Cooking time:
  None
Serves 4

1 head Romaine lettuce,
  trimmed, rinsed and
  patted dry
1 cup alfalfa sprouts
6 radishes, thinly sliced
6 shallots, finely chopped
2 tablespoons sesame oil
1 tablespoon soy sauce
1 tablespoon white wine
  vinegar
1 clove garlic, crushed

1 Arrange Romaine
lettuce on a serving
platter and top with
alfalfa sprouts, radishes,
and shallots.
2 In a small bowl stir
together sesame oil, soy
sauce, vinegar, and
garlic. Drizzle over
lettuce mixture and
serve immediately.

Gado-gado.

–TOMATOES–

Beautifully colored and unsurpassed for flavor, tomatoes are one of the most indispensable foods to have on hand in the kitchen. They may be eaten on their own, in salads or soups, or stuffed, baked, or broiled.

As well as the rounded varieties, there are also plum-shaped or Roma tomatoes, cherry tomatoes, and red or yellow pear-shaped tomatoes. Tomatoes are a valuable source of vitamins C and A and one of few vegetables whose vitamin content is not greatly diminished in cooking. Prepare just before cooking, to retain their maximum food value.

Choose plump, well-shaped tomatoes that are fairly firm-textured and brightly colored.

ON THE SIDE

Savory Tomatoes

Preparation time:
  8 minutes
Cooking time:
  None
Serves 12

12 medium tomatoes

Savory Tomatoes.

2 cups cottage
  cheese
1/2 green bell pepper,
  finely chopped
1/4 teaspoon finely
  chopped fresh basil or
  pinch dried basil,
  crushed

1 Slice the tops off
tomatoes and scoop out
the pulp with a spoon.
Invert tomato shells
onto paper towels to
drain. Set aside.
2 For filling, in a bowl
combine cottage cheese,
green pepper, and basil.
Season to taste. Spoon
filling into tomato
shells.

Note: Firm, round
tomatoes make colorful
containers for a variety
of fillings and dips.

They can be served on
their own as a first
course or snack, or
arranged on a serving
platter for a decorative
touch to the dinner
table.

Tomato Techniques

Peeling

Ready-peeled canned tomatoes make peeling unnecessary when preparing a simple casserole or soup, but there are some recipes for which freshly peeled tomatoes are invaluable.

To peel a ripe tomato, cut out the core with a small, sharp knife and score the other end to make a cross. Put the tomatoes in a bowl and pour boiling water over them, leaving them to soak for 10 seconds or till the skins start to peel back. Remove tomatoes from water, strip off the skin, then cut out the blossom at the stem end with a knife.

Seeding

It is very simple to remove the seeds from tomatoes and the little time and effort it takes will be amply rewarded in your cooking. The little seeds in tomatoes can spoil the appearance and texture of some recipes and, when cooked, may impart a slightly bitter taste to a delicately flavored dish.

All you do is cut the tomato in half crosswise and gently squeeze each half over a sieve. Scoop out any remaining seeds with a teaspoon. Discard the seeds and reserve the liquid to use in your cooking.

Making tomato pulp or concentrate

Peeled and seeded tomatoes can be cooked into a versatile pulp which can be sieved to make a soup or sauce, added to thicken a casserole, or gently reduced to a thick concentrate.

Concentrated tomato paste is the best way to freeze tomatoes as it takes up minimum space and can be reused by diluting with a little stock, water, or wine to the desired consistency.

The pulp or concentrate can be frozen in small containers of ice cube trays and then removed and stored in a plastic bag. This will keep for a year unless the tomatoes were very ripe when cooked. In this case, freeze the pulp no longer than one month.

GARNISHING TECHNIQUES

Its rich color and versatility make the tomato an ideal candidate for garnish, and here are some favorite tomato decorations.

Zigzagging

Using a sharp knife, cut through the center of the tomato in a zigzag fashion and carefully divide in two when the fruit has been cut all the way around.

Tomato rose

With a small knife, cut a slice from the base of a firm tomato and continue peeling the fruit in a spiral, taking care not to break the skin. Place the peel on a board and loosely wind it to form a neat roll

like the base of a rose. Secure it with a toothpick. Wind a second piece of skin tightly to form the center and place it in the middle of the first roll and secure with a toothpick.

Tomato tulip

Making six diagonal cuts, slice halfway down the tomato and peel the skin back with a small, sharp knife, taking care not to cut it too finely to prevent the peel from drying out.

The tomato tulip is an attractive garnish for salads, seafood platters, and glazed ham.

Red and yellow cherry tomatoes add a colorful touch to meat and salad platters. Thread onto skewers with seafood and vegetables for interesting kabobs.

MEAL IN ITSELF

Tomato and Mushroom Sauce for Pasta

Preparation time:
  10 minutes
Cooking time:
  18 minutes
Serves 4 to 6

1 1/2 pounds ripe
  tomatoes or 28-ounce
  can *whole* tomatoes,
  drained and chopped
8 ounces mushrooms,
  sliced
2 medium onions, sliced
1 clove garlic, crushed
1/3 cup finely shredded
  fresh basil or 3 to 4
  teaspoons dried basil,
  crushed
Freshly ground pepper
1 pound refrigerated
  spinach linguine or
  fettuccine or dry
  whole wheat spaghetti
Shredded fresh
  Parmesan cheese

1 If using fresh tomatoes,
peel and chop. In a large
saucepan combine
tomatoes, mushrooms,
onions, and garlic. Bring
to a boil; reduce heat.
Simmer, uncovered,
10 minutes or till
vegetables are just tender.
Stir in basil and pepper;
simmer 5 minutes more.
2 Meanwhile, cook
fresh or dry pasta in
boiling water according
to package directions or
till al dente. Drain well.
3 To serve, transfer hot
pasta to individual plates.
Spoon tomato sauce over
pasta; sprinkle with
cheese. Pass extra cheese
at the table.

Tomato and Cheese Loaf

Preparation time:
  10 to 15 minutes
Cooking time:
  15 minutes
Serves 4 to 6

16-ounce loaf French
  bread
3/4 cup French salad
  dressing
8 ounces mozzarella,
  Swiss, or muenster
  cheese, thinly sliced
3 ripe tomatoes, sliced
2 tablespoons chopped
  fresh basil

1 Halve bread
lengthwise. Scoop out
inside. Drizzle half
dressing over bottom
half of bread. Top with
half the cheese and the
tomatoes. Sprinkle with
basil. Top with
remaining cheese,
remaining dressing and
remaining bread.
2 Wrap bread tightly in
foil. Warm in 350° oven
15 minutes or chill about
30 minutes. Slice to serve.

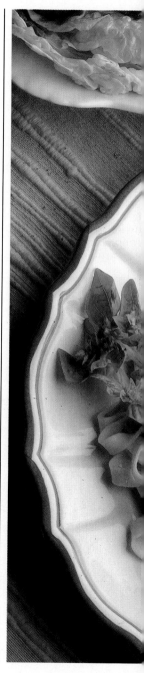

Tomato and Mushroom Sauce for Pasta.

–*Zucchini*–

Zucchini Beef Loaf

Preparation time:
  5 minutes
Cooking time:
  40 minutes
Serves 4 to 6

1 *pound lean ground beef*
1 *onion, shredded*
1 *large zucchini, shredded*
1 *clove garlic, crushed*
1/3 *cup soft bread crumbs*
2 *teaspoons soy sauce*
1 *beaten egg*

1 In a bowl combine beef, onion, zucchini, and garlic. Stir in bread crumbs, soy sauce, and egg. Mix well. In a shallow baking dish pat mixture into a 9-inch loaf.
2 Bake, uncovered, in a 350° oven for 35 to 40 minutes or till no pink remains. Drain off fat. Serve hot or cold.

On The Side

Zucchini Salad with Anchovy Dressing

Preparation time:
  6 minutes
Cooking time:
  None
Serves 4

Zucchini or courgettes (in France) are baby vegetable marrows that are harvested when immature. The best zucchini are the smallest, when the rind is tender. The flavor loses its delicacy in large zucchini, which become tough with leathery skin. The only preparation necessary is washing and slicing off the ends.

Zucchini do not need to be peeled, but if they are large, they can be peeled in strips giving the vegetable a striped appearance.

Zucchini are versatile. They can be eaten raw with dips, in salads, as a soufflé, steamed, stuffed, sautéed, baked, or made into the following mouthwatering Zucchini Beef Loaf.

Zucchini Salad with Avchovy Dressing.

4 small zucchini
2 small carrots
²/₃ cup Italian salad
  dressing
3 anchovy fillets, finely
  chopped
1 tablespoon chopped
  fresh basil or 1
  teaspoon dried, crushed
¹/₂ teaspoon sugar

1 Wash and trim zucchini and carrots. Using a vegetable peeler, cut zucchini and carrots lengthwise from top to bottom into thin ribbons. Place in a bowl of ice water for 5 minutes; drain. Arrange ribbons in a salad bowl; cover and chill till serving time.

2 For dressing, in a food processor or blender combine salad dressing, anchovies, basil, and sugar. Cover and process or blend till smooth. Pour over zucchini mixture just before serving.

INDEX

Numbers in italics represent recipe pictured.

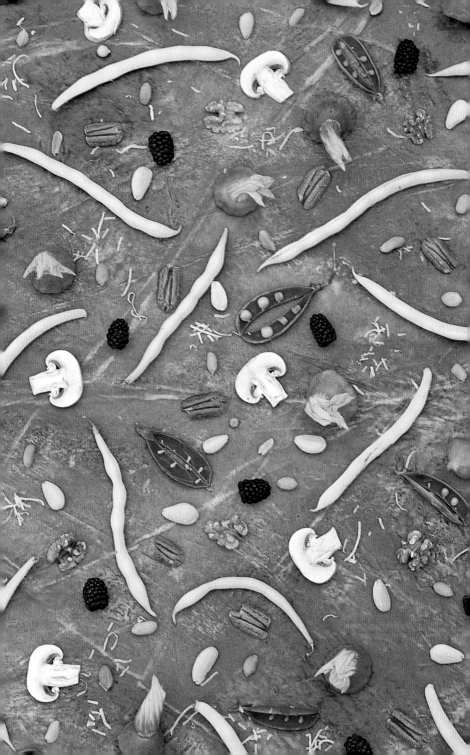